TREASURY OF LITERATURE

PRACTICE BOOK
TEACHER'S EDITION

BLUE WATERS

HARCOURT BRACE & COMPANY

Orlando   Atlanta   Austin   Boston   San Francisco   Chicago   Dallas   New York
Toronto   London

CONTENTS

Requests for permission to make copies of any part of the work should be mailed to: Permissions Department, Harcourt Brace & Company, 6277 Sea Harbor Drive, Orlando, Florida 32887-6777.

Printed in the United States of America

ISBN 0-15-302059-8

4 5 6 7 8 9 10   030   97   96   95

D.W. All Wet

Name _____

Read each sentence and the words below it. Write the word that best completes each sentence.

beach

1. Fox took a walk to the _____.

flipped   just   beach

water

2. He went down to the _____.

keep   water   just

just

3. He went in, _____ a little.

way   just   beach

stop

4. "Don't _____ there!" said Duck.

stop   beach   flipped

way

5. "Come this _____ ! she said.

way   just   stop

 Read the directions to children. Guide them through the pages or have them finish independently.

Practice Book ■ **BLUE WATERS**

Vocabulary   1

Name _____

_____

stand

6. "I will _____ right here," said Fox.

        stand   beach   just

spot

7. "This is a good _____ to be."

        keep   flipped   spot

last

8. Fox was the _____ to get wet.

        stop   last   stand

flipped

9. Look! That frog _____ over!

        flipped   beach   water

keep

10. They will _____ on playing all day.

        water   way   keep

Name _____

Fill in the story frame.

Before D.W. Got All Wet She:

felt angry

> wanted to leave

> didn't like the water

After D.W. Got All Wet She:

was happy

> stood up in the water

> played in water

> wanted to come back

 Read the directions to children. Guide them through the page or have them finish it independently.

Name _____

Read the words and sentences. Write the word that best completes each sentence.

beach	flipped	just	keep	last
spot	stand	stop	water	way

_____
beach

1. I love sand at the _____ .

_____
spot

2. I like to find a good _____ by the water.

_____
just

3. Then I _____ sit and play in the sand.

_____
stop

4. It's so much fun, I don't want to _____ .

_____
keep

5. I _____ running into the water when I get hot.

 Read the directions to children. Guide them through the page or have them finish it independently.

D.W. All Wet

Name _____

Some naming words name the **days of the week.** Begin the names of the days of the week with capital letters.

A. Write each day of the week correctly.

1. I play my drum on **monday**.

_____

Monday

_____

2. On **wednesday** I see my friends.

_____

Wednesday

_____

3. I swim on **thursday**.

_____

Thursday

_____

4. On **friday** I ride my bike.

_____

Friday

_____

 Read the directions to children. Guide them through the page or have them finish it independently.

Name _____

B. Finish the sentences. Write the names of the days of the week.

Sunday	Monday	Tuesday	Wednesday
Thursday	Friday	Saturday	

_____

1. Today is _____ .

_____
Saturday
_ _ _ _ _ _ _ _ _ _ _ _ _ _ _ _ _ _

2. We stay home on _____ and

_____
Sunday
_ _ _ _ _ _ _ _ _ _ _ _ _ _ _ _ _ _

_____ .

_____
Thursday
_ _ _ _ _ _ _ _ _ _ _ _ _ _ _ _ _ _

3. The day after Wednesday is _____ .

_____

_ _ _ _ _ _ _ _ _ _ _ _ _ _ _ _ _ _

4. The day I like best is _____ .

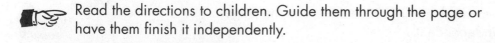 Read the directions to children. Guide them through the page or have them finish it independently.

D.W. All Wet

Name _____

Read each sentence and the words below it. Write the word that has the same vowel sound as <u>cheese</u> and that makes sense in the sentence.

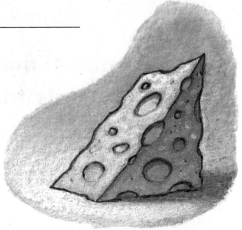

asleep

1. The baby is _____ .

   good   asleep   tree

dreaming

2. The baby is _____ .

   eat   swimming   dreaming

beach

3. We took the baby to the _____ .

   beach   teeth   water

green

4. The baby likes _____ frogs.

   seen   brown   green

sees

5. The baby _____ a duck.

   teeth   takes   sees

☞ Read the directions to children. Guide them through the page or have them finish it independently.

Name _____

Read each sentence and the words below it. Write the word that best completes each sentence.

_____
flipped

1. That frog _____ over.

flipped   flipping

_____
swimming

2. The duck is _____ .

swim   swimming

_____
digging

3. The fox is _____ a hole.

digging   dig

_____
walked

4. The chick _____ home.

walking   walked

 Read the directions to children. Guide them through the page or have them finish it independently.

D.W. ALL WET

Name _____

Complete the word in each sentence by writing the letters st or ft.

1. Our chicks can run very fa_____.

2. Six chicks were ju_____ here.

3. Five of the chicks le_____.

4. Now there is ju_____ one chick here.

5. But look what we le_____ for her.

6. This chick will eat the be_____!

 Read the directions to children. Guide them through the page or have them finish it independently.

Name _____

Read each sentence and the words below it. Write the word that best completes each sentence.

_____
felt

1. Dan Duck _____ very sad.
   felt   four   for

_____
wrote

2. Dan _____ his feelings down.
   water   wrote   would

_____ "
cry

3. "I am so sad, I could _____, he wrote.
   for   day   cry

_____
shadow

4. Then Dan saw a _____ on the water.
   shadow   why   hot

_____
boat

5. It was a _____!
   both   boat   took

 Read the directions to children. Guide them through the pages or have them finish independently.

Name _____

_____
girl

6. In the boat was a _____ .

green   girl   much

_____
visit

7. She said, "I am going to _____ my friends."

very   wide   visit

_____
want

8. "Do you _____ to come with me?"

want   what   went

_____
open

9. "We can go over the _____ sea," she said.

yes   on   open

_____
that

10. From _____ day on, Dan felt happy.

well   that   if

Name _____

Think about what Jenny saw on her trip. Fill in the chart. Write or draw what Jenny saw.

tugboats

sailboats

a bridge

On her trip at sea, Jenny saw

a big ship

sea gulls

 Read the directions to children. Guide them through the page or have them finish it independently.

••• Jenny's Journey •••

Name _____

Read the questions and the words in the boxes. Write the word that best answers each question.

1. What can you ride in on the water?

| felt | boat |

_____**boat**_____

2. What do you do when you take the lid off a box?

| want | open |

_____**open**_____

3. What do you do when you go to see a friend?

| visit | girl |

_____**visit**_____

4. What might you do when you are very sad?

| cry | that |

_____**cry**_____

 Read the directions to children. Guide them through the page or have them finish it independently.

Name _____

Some naming words name the months of the year and holidays. The names of **holidays** and **months** begin with capital letters.

1.	January	2.	February	3.	March	4.	April
5.	May	6.	June	7.	July	8.	August
9.	September	10.	October	11.	November	12.	December

A. Write the name of a month to complete each sentence.

January

1. The first month is _____.

December

2. The last month is _____.

Responses will vary.

3. My birthday is in _____.

Responses will vary.

4. The month I like best is _____.

 Read the directions to children. Guide them through the page or have them finish it independently.

Name _____

B. Write a holiday to complete each sentence.

Valentine's Day  Thanksgiving

Flag Day

_____
Flag Day
– – – – – – – – – – – – – – – – – – – –

1. We put a flag out on _____.

_____
Thanksgiving
– – – – – – – – – – – – – – – – – – – –

2. On _____ we eat a lot of food.

_____
Valentine's Day
– – – – – – – – – – – – – – – – – – – –

3. I give valentines on _____.

_____
Responses will vary.
– – – – – – – – – – – – – – – – – – – –

4. I like _____ the best

_____

– – – – – – – – – – – – – – – – – – – –

because _____.

☞ Read the directions to children. Guide them through the page or
have them finish it independently.

Name _____

Read each sentence and the words below it. Write the word that has the same vowel sound as <u>soap</u> and that makes sense in the sentence.

_____
goat

1. The _____ was eating the grass.

    goat   nose   cow

_____
boat

2. Then he saw a little _____ .

    chose   boy   boat

_____
hole

3. "Why is it in this _____ ? he said."

    lot   hole   coal

_____
coat

4. A boy in a red _____ picked the boat up.

    nose   top   coat

_____
home

5. "I need to take it _____, he said."

    home   now   soap

 Read the directions to children. Guide them through the page or have them finish it independently.

Name _____

Read the words in the box. Use those words to complete the sentences.

she	wish	shells
fish	dish	

_____
fish

1. One day Trish met a big _____ .

_____
wish

2. "Do you _____ to swim with me?" said the fish.

_____
she

3. "Yes, I do," _____ said right back.

_____ "
shells

4. "Can we look for _____? asked Trish.

_____ "
dish

5. "I keep them in a _____, said the fish to Trish.

☞ Read the directions to children. Guide them through the page or have them finish it independently.

Name _____

Complete the word in each sentence by writing the letters ft, nt, pt, or st.

ft

1. Here is a gi_____ for you.

nt

2. You can pla_____ it in the grass.

pt

3. I have ke_____ it in the sun.

st

4. At la_____ you may see it.

st

5. It is ju_____ a baby tree.

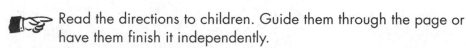 Read the directions to children. Guide them through the page or have them finish it independently.

••• SEA FROG, CITY FROG •••

Name _____

Read each sentence and the words below it. Write the word that best completes each sentence.

nice

1. Hen and Chick took a _____ walk.

    only   been   nice

"   **Hold**

2. _____ on to me," said Hen.

  Side   Hold   Only

---

side

3. "We will go to the _____ of the bushes."

    side   oh   held

---

only

4. It was _____ a little way.

  front   only   bright

---

held

5. Chick _____ on to Hen.

  held   night   side

 Read the directions to children. Guide them through the pages or have them finish independently.

Name _____

_____
front

6. "I see Duck in _____ of the bushes," said Hen.
nice   front   oh

" _____ _____ "
     Oh   **been**

7. _____ , where have you _____ ?
Front   Oh   been   bright

_____
each

8. They _____ said where they had been.
night   each   oh

_____
bright

9. Then they played until the _____ sun
went down.   hold   been   bright

_____
night

10. At last, it was _____ and time to go home.
night   each   nice

Name _____

Fill in the story frame.

Before Sea Frog and City Frog Met:

They jumped out of the pond and out of the bog.

hopped down the road

hopped up the hill

After Sea Frog and City Frog Met:

They talked and caught bugs.

took a nap

stood up and looked

went back home

 Read the directions to children. Guide them through the page or have them finish it independently.

Name _____

Read the words and sentences. Write the word that best completes each sentence.

Oh	front	been	side	
bright	hold	nice	night	held

_____
night

1. This is the _____ of the big show.

_____
front

2. Top Dog will stand in _____ of everyone.

_____
hold

3. Pup will _____ on to a horse's back.

_____
Oh

4. _____, if only I could be there!

_____
nice

5. It's going to be a very _____ show.

 Read the directions to children. Guide them through the page or have them finish it independently.

Name _____

The words **I** and **me** take the place of some naming words. Use **I** in the naming part of a sentence. Use **me** in the telling part of a sentence.

Write I̲ or m̲e̲ to complete each sentence.

_____
_ _ _ I _ _ _ _

1. _____ wanted to go to the beach.

_____
_ _ _ me _ _ _ _

2. My mother said she would take _____.

_____
_ _ _ I _ _ _ _

3. _____ asked a friend to come, too.

_____
_ _ _ me _ _ _ _

4. My friend played on the beach with _____.

_____
_ _ _ I _ _ _ _

5. She and _____ had fun at the beach.

 Read the directions to children. Guide them through the page or have them finish it independently.

Name _____

Read each sentence and the words below it. Write the word that has the same vowel sound as <u>kite</u> and that makes sense in the sentence.

bike
_____

1. Mike got a new _____.

tight   bike   wish

bright
_____

2. It is _____ red.

bright   deep   side

mine
_____ "

3. "Is that _____? asked Mike.

new   mine   sight

like
_____

4. "I _____ it a lot!"

high   saw   like

lights
_____

5. "It has _____ in front and back!"

lights   five   your

👉 Read the directions to children. Guide them through the page or have them finish it independently.

Name _____

**Complete a word in each sentence
by writing the letters ld, mp, or nd.**

_____
nd

1. Fox lives by a po_____.

_____
mp

2. It is very da_____ there.

_____
ld

3. It is very co_____, too.

_____
nd

4. Fox says, "I need to fi_____ a new home."

_____ "
mp

5. "I will find a new place to ca_____.

Read the directions to children. Guide them through the page or
have them finish it independently.

Name _____

Use clues from the sentences and from the picture to figure out the meaning of the underlined word. Fill in the circle in front of the word that completes the last sentence.

1. Look at the mallard in the lake.

    It is quacking at me.

    A mallard is a ___ .

    ● duck   ○ horse   ○ boy

2. Have you ever seen a very big bike like that one?

    It is gigantic!

    Gigantic means ___ .

    ○ very small   ○ blue   ● very big

3. The clown looks very cheerful.

    He looks this happy every time I see him.

    Cheerful means ___ .

    ● happy   ○ sad   ○ fast

☞ Read the directions to children. Guide them through the page or have them finish it independently.

Name _____

Read the words in the box. Write the word or words that best complete each sentence.

flip	flipped	flipping
hop	hopped	hopping

_____
hopping

1. Rita was _____ on one leg.

_____
hopped

2. She _____ all the way home.

_____
flipped

3. Then she _____ right over.

_____
flipping

4. She was _____ again and again.

_____   _____
flip   **hop**

5. "Rita, let's _____ and _____ together."

👉 Read the directions to children. Guide them through the page or have them finish it independently.

Name _____

Write the word or words from the box that best complete each sentence.

we're	about	knows
safe	need	goes

about

1. I go swimming just _____ every day.

need

2. I _____ my cap on in the water.

goes

3. My dog _____ in the water, too.

knows   **safe**

4. He _____ he's _____ with me.

we're

5. Ruff knows _____ best friends.

 Read the directions to children. Guide them through the pages or have them finish independently.

Name _____

_____
I've

6. _____ always wanted a dog like Ruff.

_____
wait

7. I had to _____ till I was big enough.

_____
you're

8. I know _____ happy you have a dog, too.

_____
next

9. The _____ time you come, bring your dog.

_____
may

10. Our dogs _____ get to be good friends.

Name _____

Think about what happened after Punky and Grampy got in the boat. List what happened in order on the flowchart. The pictures will help you remember.

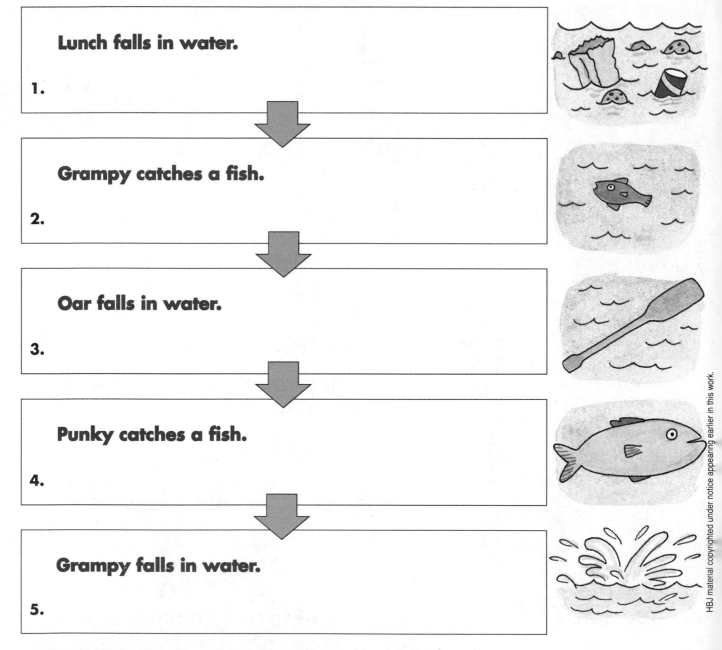

Lunch falls in water.

1.

Grampy catches a fish.

2.

Oar falls in water.

3.

Punky catches a fish.

4.

Grampy falls in water.

5.

 Read the directions to children. Guide them through the page or have them finish it independently.

Name _____

Read each sentence and the words below it. Write the word that best completes each sentence.

_____
We're
_____

1. _____ going for a bike ride.

We're   I've   Wanted

_____
need

2. I _____ to put this on.

you're   may   need

_____
about

3. It looks just _____ right for you.

next   about   wanted

_____
safe

4. Now you will be _____.

safe   goes   wait

 Read the directions to children. Guide them through the page or have them finish it independently.

Name _____

The words **he**, **she**, and **it** take the place of
some naming words.

**A. Write the words that mean the same as the
underlined word. Circle the matching picture.**

1. Sally got the boat out.
   <u>Sh</u>e put it in the water.

   _____
                Sally

   <u>She</u> means _____ .

2. The boy played with the boat.
   <u>H</u>e likes boats.

   _____
               the boy

   <u>He</u> means _____ .

3. A fish jumped up.
   <u>I</u>t wanted to see the boat.

   _____
               a fish

   <u>It</u> means _____ .

 Read the directions to children. Guide them through the page or
have them finish it independently.

Name _____

B. Read each sentence. Write the word that can take the place of the underlined word or words.

He	She	It

_____
She

1. <u>Anna</u> walked to the park. _____

_____
He

2. <u>Father</u> saw a duck. _____

_____
It

3. <u>The duck</u> looked little. _____

_____
She

4. <u>Anna</u> fed the duck. _____

_____
It

5. <u>The duck</u> ate the food. _____

☞ Read the directions to children. Guide them through the page or have them finish it independently.

Using *He, She,* and *It*

Name _____

Write the contraction for the underlined words. The words in the box will help you.

You're	we've	We're
I've	You'd	I'd

1. <u>We are</u> at the beach.

   We're

2. <u>You are</u> swimming.

   You're

3. <u>I have</u> been digging.

   I've

4. <u>I would</u> like to stay here.

   I'd

5. <u>You would</u> like to stay, too.

   You'd

6. What fun <u>we have</u> had!

   we've

 Read the directions to children. Guide them through the page or have them finish it independently.

••• PUNKY GOES FISHING •••

Name _____

Look at each picture. Then complete the sentences.

1. The hen is the _____**chick's**_____ mother.

       chick's   horse's

2. It is _____**Ida's**_____ bike.

     mouse's   Ida's

3. This is the _____**mouse's**_____ cheese.

     chick's   mouse's

4. He is the _____**baby's**_____ father.

     hen's   baby's

5. This is the _____**horse's**_____ home.

     horse's   tree's

 Read the directions to children. Guide them through the page or have them finish it independently.

PUNKY GOES FISHING

Name _____

Read the sentences. Write the word or words that best complete the last sentence.

1. Pig asked his friends to come over. His

"_____**Hello**_____"

friends came. Pig said, _____.

Hello   Go away

---

2. Pat is hot. She wants to go to the beach.

_____**dig**_____

Pat will _____.

nap   dig

---

3. "May I play my drum?" asked Duck. "Not now,"

_____**wait**_____

said Mother. Duck must _____.

wait   jump

 Read the directions to children. Guide them through the page or have them finish it independently.

HBJ material copyrighted under notice appearing earlier in this work.

Name _____

Read each sentence and the words below it. Write the word that best completes each sentence.

whale

1. Baby _____ was swimming by his mother.

   laughed   along   whale

along

2. They were swimming _____ side by side.

   along   real   sail

3. The whales saw some men on a boat.

sail

"They like to _____ by and see us," said Mother.

sail   someday   along

real

4. "Look!" cried a man. "Those are _____ whales."

laughed   along   real

 Read the directions to children. Guide them through the pages or have them finish independently.

Name _____

_____ "
river

5. "I've never seen a whale in our _____ .

real　　　river　　　sail

---

6. "I've never seen a boat like that!

_____
sail

I want to _____ in a boat," said Baby.

laughed　　　sail　　　whale

" _____
Someday

7. _____ I will!"

Along　　　River　　　Someday

_____
laughed

8. "You're a silly whale!" _____ Mother.

sail　　　real　　　laughed

Name _____

Complete the chart by writing what Little Bear and Owl do and what they pretend to do.

What Little Bear and Owl Really Do:	What Little Bear and Owl Pretend to Do:
Little Bear is really **Little Bear**	He pretends to be **Father Bear**
They go fishing at the **river**	They go fishing on the **ocean**
They sit on a **log**	They sit on a **boat**
They catch a **small fish**	They catch a whale and an **octopus**

 Read the directions to children. Guide them through the page or have them finish it independently.

Name _____

Read the words in the box. Write the word that best completes each sentence.

along	**laughed**	**real**
river	**Someday**	

_____ "
                    Someday

1. Pig said, _____, I'd like to be a duck."

_____
                    along

2. "I love the way ducks sail _____ on the water."

_____
                    laughed

3. Pig's mother _____.

_____
                    real

4. "You can't be a _____ duck."

_____ "
                    river

5. "Just play in the _____.

☞ Read the directions to children. Guide them through the page or have them finish it independently.

Name _____

Describing words tell about naming words.

A. Circle each describing word. Then write it.

(yellow) boat

yellow

(brown) bear

brown

(big) hat

big

(wet) frog

wet

(happy) bear

happy

(blue) water

blue

 Read the directions to children. Guide them through the page or have them finish it independently.

Name _____

B. Write a describing word to complete each sentence.

long	green	blue

_____
blue
- - - - - - - - - - - - - - - - - - - -

1. The bear has on a _____ hat.

_____
long
- - - - - - - - - - - - - - - - - - - -

2. He has a _____ fishing rod.

_____
green
- - - - - - - - - - - - - - - - - - - -

3. The _____ fish is smiling.

C. Write a sentence about the picture. Use a describing word. Circle it.

_____
Responses will vary.
- - - - - - - - - - - - - - - - - - - -

_____

_____

_____

Read the directions to children. Guide them through the page or have them finish it independently.

Name _____

Read the words. Write number **1** by the word that is first in ABC order. Write **2** by the word that is second. Write **3** by the word that is third. The first one is done for you.

ABCDEFGHIJKLMNOPQRSTUVWXYZ

1. ⭐ __1__ along   __3__ mouse   __2__ every

2. __2__ laughed   __1__ father   __3__ water

3. __3__ whale   __1__ real   __2__ shouted

4. __3__ river   __2__ looked   __1__ grass

5. __2__ nap   __1__ hold   __3__ sail

6. __1__ cut   __3__ web   __2__ lot

7. __3__ want   __1__ goes   __2__ know

8. __1__ about   __3__ night   __2__ each

 Read the directions to children. Guide them through the page or have them finish it independently.

Name _____

Complete a word in each sentence by writing the letters <u>sh</u> or <u>wh</u>.

wh

1. "Duck, _____at is this?" asked Mouse.

sh

2. "Come here and _____ow me," said Duck.

sh

3. "It looks like _____ells, put together."

wh

4. "Do you know _____y that is?" asked Mouse.

Wh

5. "No, but let's give it to our friend, _____ale," Duck said.

Read the directions to children. Guide them through the page or have them finish it independently.

Name _____

Read the words in the box. Use those words to complete the sentences. Then circle the picture that the sentence tells about.

bone	hole	road	boat

_____
bone

1. The dog has a _____ .

_____
road

2. He walks down the _____ .

_____
hole

3. See the _____ he's digging.

_____
boat

4. The dog wants to get a _____ .

👉 Read the directions to children. Guide them through the page or have them finish it independently.

Name _____

Read each sentence and the words below it. Write the word that best completes each sentence.

woman

1. This _____ is named Bess.

   planted   woman   laid

these

2. Bess loves _____ hens.

   woman   these   egg

made

3. Bess _____ the hen house.

   made   egg   these

planted

4. Look at the flowers she _____ all around.

   planted   cake   these

 Read the directions to children. Guide them through the pages or have them finish independently.

Name _____

_____
ate

5. Bess saw that each hen _____ well every day.

ate   woman   cake

_____

_____
cake

6. She surprised the hens with _____ sometimes.

ate   woman   cake

_____

_____
grew

7. The hens _____ very fast.

made   these   grew

_____

_____
laid

8. That happy little hen just _____ an egg.

laid   these   woman

_____

_____
egg

9. She is giving the _____ to her friend Bess.

grew   made   egg

Name _____

Many things happened before Mack ate the cake.
Complete the flowchart by writing the missing words.
The pictures will help you.

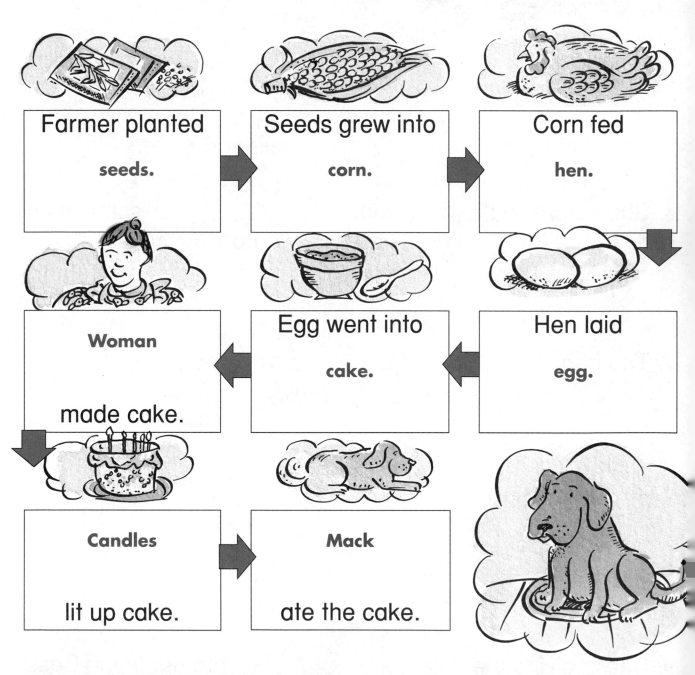

Farmer planted **seeds.**	Seeds grew into **corn.**	Corn fed **hen.**
Woman made cake.	Egg went into **cake.**	Hen laid **egg.**
Candles lit up cake.	**Mack** ate the cake.	

Read the directions to children. Guide them through the page or
have them finish it independently.

Name _____

Read each sentence. Write a word from
the box to complete each sentence.

grew	these	woman
ate	cake	laid
made	egg	planted

_____
made

1. Four friends _____ their home in a tree.

_____
these

2. I used to love to see _____ friends play all day.

_____
ate

3. Each night, they went home and _____ together.

_____
laid

4. Then they _____ down their toys and went to sleep.

_____
grew

5. These four friends _____ up to be very happy.

👉 Read the directions to children. Guide them through the page or
have them finish it independently.

Name _____

Some **describing words** tell how people feel.

A. **W**rite a describing word from the box to tell how each person feels.

happy	surprised	sleepy	sad

_____

sleepy

- - - - - - - - - - - - - - - -

1. _____

_____

surprised

- - - - - - - - - - - - - - - -

2. _____

_____

sad

- - - - - - - - - - - - - - - -

3. _____

_____

happy

- - - - - - - - - - - - - - - -

4. _____

 Read the directions to children. Guide them through the page or have them finish it independently.

Name _____

B. **Look at the picture. Then read each sentence. Write a describing word to tell how each person feels.**

_____
sad
- - - - - - - - - - - -

1. The father held the _____ baby.
   sad   happy

_____

_____
happy
- - - - - - - - - - - -

2. The _____ boy played with a boat.
   mad   happy

_____

_____
hungry
- - - - - - - - - - - -

3. The _____ girl asked for cake.
   scared   hungry

_____

_____
sleepy
- - - - - - - - - - - -

4. The _____ mother took a nap.
   sleepy   hungry

 Read the directions to children. Guide them through the page or have them finish it independently.

Name _____

Complete a word in each sentence by writing the letters gg, dd, tt, or zz.

gg

1. Don was eating an e_____ by the tree.

zz

2. There was a bu_____ from the tree.

dd

3. That's o_____.

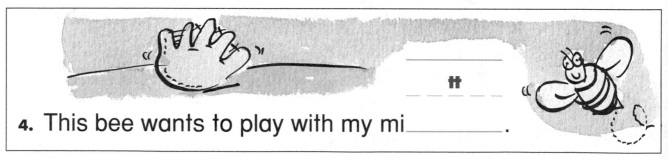

tt

4. This bee wants to play with my mi_____.

👉 Read the directions to children. Guide them through the page or have them finish it independently.

Name _____

Name each picture. Write the word that
has the same beginning sounds as the
picture name.

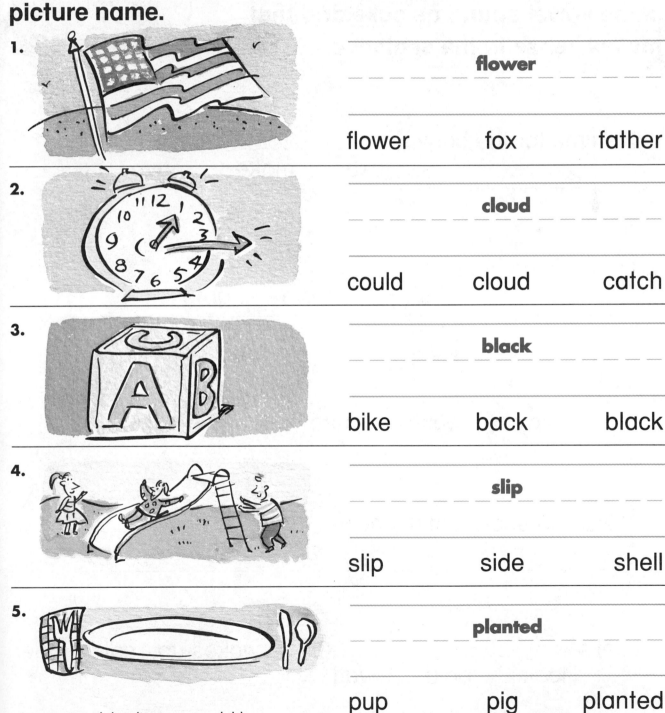

1. **flower**

   flower　　fox　　father

2. **cloud**

   could　　cloud　　catch

3. **black**

   bike　　back　　black

4. **slip**

   slip　　side　　shell

5. **planted**

   pup　　pig　　planted

Read the directions to children.
Guide them through the page or have them finish it independently.

Name _____

Read each sentence and the words below it. Write the word that has the same vowel sound as <u>cake</u> and that makes sense in the sentence.

take

1. It's time for the baby to _____ a nap.

   take   make   have

gate

2. Clay comes in the _____.

   stay   room   gate

wake

3. "Can I _____ the baby?" asked Clay.

   way   wake   here

train

4. "I want to show him my new _____!

   train   bike   say

wait

5. "Let's _____ till he wakes up," said Father.

   look   paid   wait

☞ Read the directions to children. Guide them through the page or have them finish it independently.

Name _____

Read each sentence and the words
below it. Write the word that best
completes each sentence.

_____ **has** _____

1. Jo _____ a lion, a chick, and a frog.

    food   think   has

_____ **were** _____

2. Last night they _____ all on the shelf.

    shelf   were   any

_____ **doesn't** _____

3. Jo _____ see her lion.

    food   doesn't   having

_____ **shelf** _____

4. It is not up on the _____ .

    shelf   has   always

_____ **before** _____ "

5. "It was here _____ , says Jo.

    biting   liked   before

 Read the directions to children. Guide them through the pages or
have them finish independently.

Name _____

always

6. "I _____ set it here on the shelf."

any   before   always

having   **biting**

7. The cat is _____ fun _____ the lion.

doesn't   having   biting   any

think

8. "What do you _____ you are doing?" says Jo.

food   think   shelf

any

9. "You can't do that _____ more!"

having   any   liked

food

10. "That lion is not your _____! says Jo.

food   think   shelf

LIONEL AT LARGE

Name _____

Fill in the story frame.

Lionel's First Problem

He doesn't want to eat his green beans.

How Lionel Solves the Problem

He says that he doesn't have a vegetable shelf.

Lionel's Second Problem

He can't have dessert unless he eats his green beans.

How Lionel Solves the Problem

He eats his green beans.

 Read the directions to children. Guide them through the page or have them finish it independently.

Name _____

Read each sentence. Write a word from
the box to complete each one.

always	before	having
think	shelf	food

_____
food

1. I eat any kind of _____ .

_____
think

2. I can't _____ of any food I don't like.

_____
always

3. Cheese has _____ been a food that I like.

_____
having

4. I like _____ eggs in the morning.

_____
shelf

5. What foods do you like to have on your _____ ?

☞ Read the directions to children. Guide them through the page or
have them finish it independently.

Name _____

Some describing words tell about **size** and **shape**.

Answer each question with a describing word.

1. What shape is the ball?

_____
round
_____

square   round

2. What shape is the book?

_____
square
_____

3. What size is the bird?

_____
little
_____

little   big

4. What size is the cow?

_____
big
_____

 Read the directions to children. Guide them through the page or have them finish it independently.

Name _____

Read the sentences. Drop the <u>e</u> from the underlined word and add **-ed** or **-ing** so that the word makes sense in the second sentence. Write the new word.

> lik~~e~~ + ed = liked
>
> bit~~e~~ + ing = biting

1. My friends <u>love</u> to eat cheese.

loved

They have always _____ it.

2. We will <u>have</u> cheese and other food.

having

We are _____ the food soon.

3. My father likes to <u>make</u> our food.

making

He is _____ it right now.

 Read the directions to children. Guide them through the page or have them finish it independently.

••• LIONEL AT LARGE •••

Name _____

Use clues from the sentence to figure out the meaning of the underlined word. Circle the picture that shows the meaning.

1. Four friends ate a big <u>watermelon</u> together.

2. They saw <u>trout</u> swimming up the river.

3. The friends picked some bright red <u>tulips</u> that grew in the grass.

4. Then the friends rode their <u>bicycles</u> home.

 Read the directions to children. Guide them through the page or have them finish it independently.

Name _____

Read each sentence and the words below it. Write the word that best completes each sentence.

_____ "

flew

1. Sandy said, "I saw a pig that _____!

 after   flew   many

climbed

2. "The pig _____ up the hill."

 climbed   better   some

"_____

After

3. _____ that, it jumped off and flew around!"

Something   Many   After

something

4. "It was _____ to see!"

 something   should   their

some

5. "That was _____ pig!"

 ever   some   around

 Read the directions to children. Guide them through the pages or have them finish independently.

Name _____

_____   _____
should   **better**

6. Sandy _____ know _____ than that.

   climbed   should   better   around

_____

_____
ever

7. Pigs don't _____ fly.

   some   ever   their

_____

_____
around

8. Look _____, and you'll see.

   around   flew   climbed

_____

_____
many

9. How _____ flying pigs are there?

   after   better   many

_____

_____
their

10. Pigs fly only in _____ dreams.

    their   something   should

Name _____

What things do Frog and Toad do to keep from eating more cookies? List those things in order on the flowchart. The pictures will help you.

put cookies in box

tie box with string

put box on high shelf

take box down

feed cookies to birds

 Read the directions to children. Guide them through the page or have them finish it independently.

Name _____

Read each sentence. Write a word from
the box to complete each one.

| after | around | ever | many |
| should | some | something | their |

1. I've got _____ **something** _____ .

2. I looked all _____ **around** _____ for it.

3. At last, _____ **after** _____ a lot of looking, I saw it.

4. Did you _____ **ever** _____ see a pup as nice as this?

👉 Read the directions to children. Guide them through the page or
have them finish it independently.

Name _____

Some describing words tell how things **taste** and **smell**.

| smoky | salty | sweet | sour |

A. Write a describing word to complete each sentence.

_____
sweet
- - - - - - - - - - - - - - - - -

1. He smells a _____ flower.

_____
smoky
- - - - - - - - - - - - - - - - -

2. I smell a _____ fire.

_____
sour
- - - - - - - - - - - - - - - - -

3. She eats a _____ lemon.

_____
salty
- - - - - - - - - - - - - - - - -

4. She eats some _____ ham.

 Read the directions to children. Guide them through the page or have them finish it independently.

Name _____

B. Read each sentence. Write the describing word for each taste or smell.

salty

1. Do you like salty crackers? _____

sour

2. These are sour grapes. _____

smoky

3. What is that smoky smell? _____

fresh

4. Smell the fresh air. _____

C. Write a sentence. Use a describing word for taste or smell.

_____

Responses will vary.

_____

_____

 Read the directions to children. Guide them through the page or have them finish it independently.

Name _____

Name each picture. Write the word that has the
same beginning sounds as the picture name
and that makes sense in the sentence.

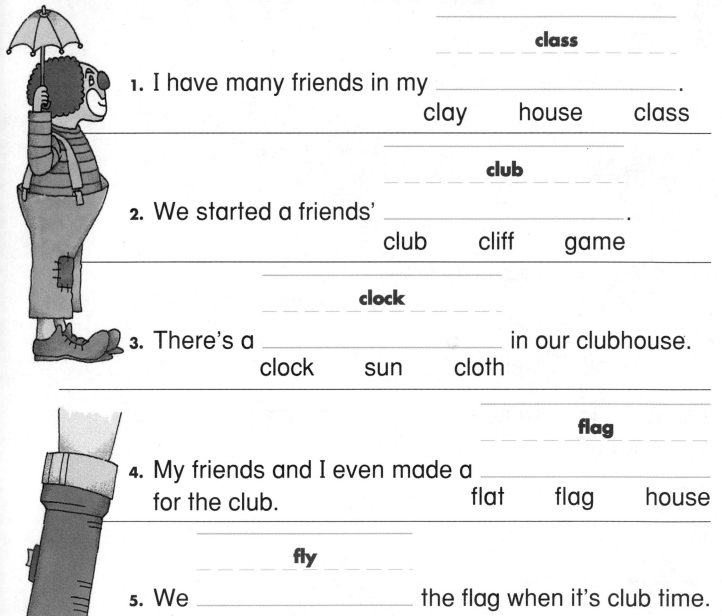

class

1. I have many friends in my _____.

          clay   house   class

club

2. We started a friends' _____.

       club   cliff   game

clock

3. There's a _____ in our clubhouse.

   clock   sun   cloth

flag

4. My friends and I even made a _____
for the club.   flat   flag   house

fly

5. We _____ the flag when it's club time.

   like   fly   flat

 Read the directions to children. Guide them through the page or
have them finish it independently.

Name _____

Read the sentences. Drop the <u>e</u> from the underlined word and add <u>-ed</u> or <u>-ing</u> so that the word makes sense in the second sentence. Write the new word.

> lov~~e~~ + ed = loved
>
> mak~~e~~ + ing = making

1. Mike will <u>have</u> something to eat.

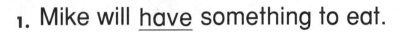

_____
having

He is _____ something to eat.

2. Mike will <u>take</u> his dog to the river.

_____
taking

He is _____ his dog to the river now.

3. They <u>like</u> to play together.

_____
liked

They have always _____ to play together.

☞ Read the directions to children. Guide them through the page or have them finish it independently.

Name _____

Number the words in ABC order. Then write the words in order to make sentences.

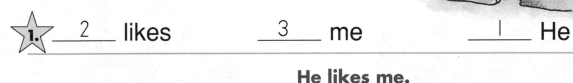

1. ___2___ likes   ___3___ me   ___1___ He

_____

He likes me.

_____

2. ___1___ Darrell   ___3___ playing   ___2___ is

_____

Darrell is playing.

_____

3. ___3___ outside   ___1___ Anna   ___2___ goes

_____

Anna goes outside.

_____

4. ___3___ Mouse   ___1___ Cat   ___2___ finds

_____

Cat finds Mouse.

_____

Read the directions to children. Guide them through the page or have them finish it independently.

Name _____

Read each sentence and the words below it. Write the word or words that best complete each sentence.

rang

1. Anna sat and _____ the bell on her bike.

    door   rang   two

dear "

2. "What's wrong, _____? asked Father.

    three   perhaps   dear

nobody

3. "There's _____ to play with," said Anna.

    rang   door   nobody

two   **three**

4. "Ask _____ or _____ friends over."

    two perhaps   rang three

 Read the directions to children. Guide them through the pages or have them finish independently.

Name _____

" _____
Perhaps

5. _____ Lucas and Tara can play," said Father.
Three   Perhaps   Nobody

_____

_____ "
children

6. "There are some _____! said Anna.
yourselves   children   door

_____

_____ "
door

7. "They are just coming out the _____!
door   nobody   perhaps

_____

_____ "
yourselves

8. "Good!" said Father. "Enjoy _____!
dear   rang   yourselves

THE DOORBELL RANG

Name _____

Complete the flowchart by writing how many children were at the door each time. Write how many of the twelve cookies each child got.

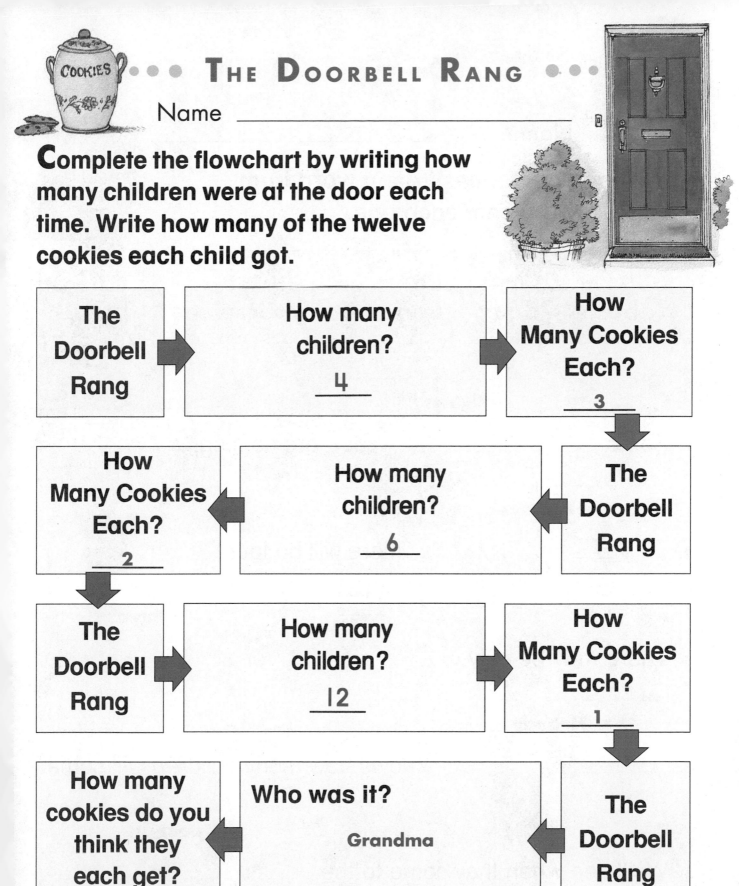

| The Doorbell Rang | ➡ | How many children? **4** | ➡ | How Many Cookies Each? **3** |

| How Many Cookies Each? **2** | ⬅ | How many children? **6** | ⬅ | The Doorbell Rang |

| The Doorbell Rang | ➡ | How many children? **12** | ➡ | How Many Cookies Each? **1** |

| How many cookies do you think they each get? Responses will vary. | ⬅ | Who was it? *Grandma* _____ | ⬅ | The Doorbell Rang |

 Read the directions to children. Guide them through the page or have them finish it independently.

THE DOORBELL RANG

Name _____

Read each sentence. Write a word from the box to complete each one.

door	two	three	children
Nobody	dear	Perhaps	yourselves

children

1. Some _____ are coming.

Perhaps

2. _____ there will be four.

two   **three**

3. There may be only _____ or _____.

Nobody

4. _____ knows how many children will come.

door

5. We'll see when they come to the _____.

 Read the directions to children. Guide them through the page or have them finish it independently.

••• THE DOORBELL RANG •••

Name _____

Some describing words tell **how many.**
Some describing words name **colors.**

A. Write a color word to complete each sentence.

_____
orange
- - - - - - - - - - - - - - - - -

1. The _____ cheese is very good.

_____
red
- - - - - - - - - - - - - - - - -

2. Do you like _____ apples?

_____
white
- - - - - - - - - - - - - - - - -

3. Where are the _____ eggs?

_____
brown
- - - - - - - - - - - - - - - - -

4. They are in the _____ basket.

Read the directions to children. Guide them through the page or
have them finish it independently.

Name _____

1 one	2 two	3 three	4 four	5 five
6 six	7 seven	8 eight	9 nine	10 ten

B. Write a number word to complete each sentence.

_____
one
- - - - - - - - - -

1. There is _____ apple in the first box.

_____
three
- - - - - - - - - -

2. I will eat the _____ yellow apples.

_____
five
- - - - - - - - - -

3. Do you want the _____ green ones?

_____
ten
- - - - - - - - - -

4. There are _____ red apples in the last box.

 Read the directions to children. Guide them through the page or have them finish it independently.

Name _____

Write the word that has the same vowel sound as the picture name and makes sense in the sentence.

fly

bike

1. I am glad that I have a _____ .

   friend   dry   bike

ride

2. It is a lot of fun to _____ .

   see   ride   might

light

3. My bike has a _____ in front.

   light   seat   by

night

4. The light is for riding at _____ .

   home   night   shy

my

5. I love to ride _____ bike.

   by   ripe   my

👉 Read the directions to children. Guide them through the page or have them finish it independently.

Name _____

Read the sentences. Write the word or words that best complete the last sentence.

1. Father took Jim to the river. Jim saw a duck.

" _____ "
Quack

The duck said, _____.

Quack   Count   Sail

2. Mona liked to keep shells. She saw a nice

_____
take it

shell. Mona will _____.

take it   go away

3. My father got out some eggs. He put them

_____
eat

in a pan. He is going to _____.

play   eat   run

 Read the directions to children. Guide them through the page or have them finish it independently.